The History and
of
Brownsea Is

C000269737

A Fast Facts Guide

Welcome to Brownsea Island

Stepping ashore on Brownsea Island you will find yourself in one of the most enchanting places in all England; a place which is teeming with wildlife, and rich in flora.

As you wander around this beautiful island you will come across many special sights, including the majestic peacocks and possibly the shy red squirrels.

If you are interested in history then you have come to the right place, for Brownsea Island has a rich and varied past. There is so much to do and learn on your visit that you certainly won't be bored.

Through this little book, you can look at Brownsea through different eyes, the eyes of those who have shaped it down through the ages, of those people who have lived and worked on the island, and loved it as much as we do today.

As you explore this intriguing island you might start to question the how?... when?... and... why?

The following pages will perhaps help to answer those questions. Through the illustrations by James Langan and the flashbacks, the people from the island's past come alive, and give a real insight into the History and Mystery of Brownsea Island.

The last five pages in the book concentrate on the woodland, heathland, lagoon, reed beds and seashore: a map on each page shows you where they may be found; what to look out for, and when.

Although the island is only a mile and a half long and a mile wide, you might find that one visit is not enough to soak up all the interesting aspects of Brownsea Island.

Hold tight for a fascinating journey as you go back through the centuries!

Question: When did people first settle on Brownsea Island?
Answer: At least by 500B.C.

Question: Has Brownsea Island ever been a Holy Island?
Answer: Yes.

Flashback: You find yourself being taken way back through the centuries to the year 890. A tapping sound can be heard. As your eyes adjust to the light you notice a man dressed in long dark clothes engrossed in his work; you watch as he puts the finishing touches to a planished and chased gold cross. Distant chanting voices can be heard through the open oak door.
You realise that you are in a small spartan chapel, and begin to feel anxious as a robed and hooded man approaches you. You sigh with relief when he turns towards the worker whom he calls Brother Joseph.

He seems to be chastising him for not having finished his task. Putting his tools down, Brother Joseph proudly hands the golden cross to his Brother, who then places it at the centre of the humble altar.
Whoosh: Suddenly you are pushed forward in time to the year 1015, and find yourself kneeling at the altar; a monk beckons you to follow him outside. As you obey, you hear sounds of pounding footsteps and the voices of raging men; looking towards the beach you are horrified to see forty or fifty Vikings charging towards you! The monk directs you to a hidden hollow, where you observe terrible deeds. The chapel is attacked and set on fire; monks flee in all directions; many are killed and wounded. After the invaders have left you pick your way through the carnage. One dying monk is crying out in a tongue you don't understand; as you near his badly beaten body he sighs his last, and from out of his loosened hand falls the gold cross.

Records show that people have lived on Brownsea Island for the past 2,500 years. An oak log boat recovered off the island, and shiny black pottery made from the local clay, found on the island, gives evidence of this.

Further discoveries show that the Romans were also here.

During the 9th century it was the monks from Cerne Abbey near Dorchester who had a chapel and hermitage built on Brownsea Island. The chapel was dedicated to St Andrew, the patron saint of fishermen.

In 1015 Viking longships carrying Cnut and his army arrived on our shores. The soldiers wreaked havoc throughout the countryside, killing, maiming and stealing all that was valuable. They devastated the monasteries, including Cerne Abbey and the chapel on Brownsea Island. When Cnut became King of England, the pillaged goods from Cerne Abbey were returned.

For the next 350 years the island belonged to the monks of Cerne Abbey who had the right of wreckage from goods washed ashore. Evidence of this period was found in the 20th century when remains of a medieval cemetery were found.

Despite the Viking invasion, the island has seen many goods deeds: for example, during the Middle Ages a hermit built a shelter on the island and lit a beacon to guide ships at night.

Brownsea got its name in the days of Edward the Confessor. The name Brownsea means Bruno; in more modern times it became Branksea; then in the 20th century, Brownsea.

Question: When was the castle built and by whom?
Answer: In 1545 by local merchants, after
**   encouragement from Henry VIII.**

Flashback: *As the years unwind you find yourself on the south eastern side of Brownsea Island. The morning sunshine dances on the vibrant blue water and seagulls cry overhead. It is 1545. A large white square building is under construction and you are surrounded by many working men. Watch out! A huge wooden beam skims over your head; the men scramble to prevent it falling, their voices high pitched and urgent.*

A boat pulls in by the jetty; you watch as huge blocks of stone are loaded onto a large barrow and wheeled to the building site. A second boat arrives, and five elegantly dressed merchants disembark. After pausing and surveying the building, they walk towards it, talking all the while. Stopping close to you, one of the men, who speaks in a rather superior tone, says that the king will be pleased indeed at the quality of work. Another, after looking closely at the newly arrived stone, says proudly that he was able to get the stone at a good rate, as his cousin is in charge of the quarry.

By 1540, Cerne Abbey, along with all other religious foundations had been closed and taken over by the crown. After a threatened invasion by the French, local merchants, with encouragement from King Henry VIII, built the castle on Brownsea Island, its position well placed to protect or control the entrance to Poole Harbour. Many other coastal forts were built along the English Channel at this time. Poole burgesses paid for the chalk, stone, and a pair of wheels for the guns. The building, a substantial blockhouse, had walls 44 feet (13.4112 metres) long, over 9 feet (2.7432 metres) wide, a moat on three sides, and a drawbridge, which was 23 feet (7.0104 metres) long. As the Spanish threat increased, strengthening the castle was always under review, and in 1551 the walls of the blockhouse were raised: should the enemy occupy the hill behind the castle, the gun crews would otherwise be seen and vulnerable. In 1588 the Spanish Armada engaged the English fleet between Portland and the Isle of Wight, but were fortunately beaten off.

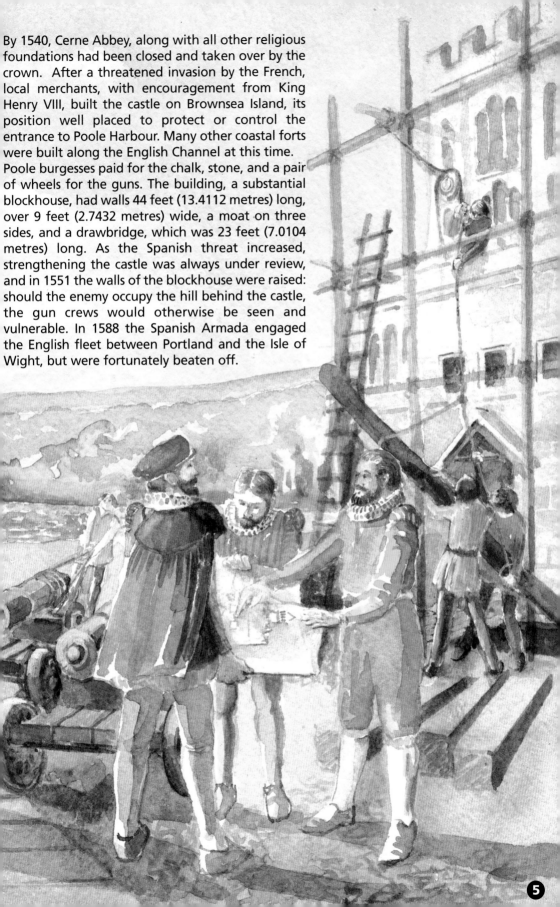

Question: What happened to the castle when the king died?

Answer: *It was inherited by Queen Elizabeth 1.*

Flashback:
Back you go once more; there is a chill in the air, and it feels like autumn. The year is 1576. Ouch! Something pricks your leg, and your feet sink into the sandy soil. You are on the south side of the island surrounded by heather, gorse and couch grass, all of which are covered in cobwebs, which glisten with the dew. Then, hearing the rustle of feet, you look up to see a man and woman walking near by, deep in conversation. You strain to hear what they are saying, but only catch the merest of whispers.

You notice that the lady, who has her back to you, has an exquisite high ruffled dress. The gentleman is dressed in a fine costume, adorned with gold buttons which sparkle in the morning sun; the feathers in his cap bend in the gentle breeze. He is holding a large bunch of keys. You observe them laughing together and realise that they are perfectly at ease with each other.

After Henry VIII died in 1547, the island was passed on to his son, Edward VI, who reigned for six years. Following Edward's premature death, Henry's daughter Mary I came to the throne until 1558, when her sister Elizabeth I became queen. In 1561 after complaints by the mayor and burgesses of Poole about the dilapidated condition of the castle, repairs were made and a gunner appointed, who carried out the burgesses' orders in return for a salary. At this time a permanent guard of six men were placed by Poole.

The mayor and burgesses of Poole were unhappy once more, when, in 1576, Queen Elizabeth 1 gave Brownsea Island to one of her favourites, Christopher Hatton. Elizabeth had already sold him Corfe Castle, and made him Lord Admiral of Purbeck. Christopher, who was knighted in 1577, used the castle guns to force all ships to pay him a toll, and therefore was unpopular with the locals and seafaring folk.

Question: Who owned Brownsea Island during the 17th and 18th centuries?

Answer: *A succession of MPs, including 'Mad Benson'.*

Flashback: *As the years unwind, you find yourself shivering with the cold. It is 1758: you are surrounded by darkness and feel afraid. Whispering voices seem to be everywhere: then, as your eyes adjust to the light you realise you are in a wood and the tall tress are swaying and whispering around you. Suddenly an eerie laughter breaks the silence; you turn to see a naked man dancing around a fire, his face contorted and manic. Your fear intensifies when a desperate scream fills the air. You beg to leave this time.*

Whoosh: What a relief. You feel warm and find yourself outside a charming cottage; the awful screams have faded and been replaced by the call of many pheasants, which surround you. The year is 1798. A pretty girl beckons you to follow her, and soon you find yourself on the castle terrace, where many men are working. You watch as a huge gun is manoeuvred into place alongside two others. Moving closer to the men you catch some of their conversation. A well built man nods towards the guns and says in a rather frightened voice that they may ward off seaborne invaders but they can't keep out the demon screams, which he heard again last night. A slight, grey haired man tells him not to dwell on it, and that they'd better get the other gun in place before the master gets back.

The island, which had often been neglected in the past, was transformed by various wealthy owners over the following centuries. The first of these was Sir Robert Clayton, a City of London merchant. He bought the island during the Commonwealth, and was the first of a succession of MPs to own Brownsea Island. His heirs sold the island to William Benson MP, around 1726.

Benson was a philosopher, poet and architect who replaced Sir Christopher Wren as Surveyor-General of the King's works. A knowledgeable botanist, he planted a variety of trees on the island.

It was Benson who converted the castle into a home. As the castle was on crown property, the Mayor of Poole wrote to the king, telling him his concerns about the conversion. Attempts to stop Benson failed, and the castle never housed ordnance again.

Benson, an eccentric, was given to fits of madness and became known as 'Mad Benson'. He dabbled in black magic, and locals said that he used to dance naked around a fire, and that screams heard at night were from a young servant girl who was sacrificed in one of his rituals. Over the following years some folk have been spooked by unexplained screams coming from the woods.

By 1765 the island was owned by Sir Humphrey Sturt, a local landowner who rebuilt the castle on a grand scale. He spent over £50,000 on the adjoining ornamental gardens, and created the two freshwater lakes. He also pioneered new ideas on crop rotation and shipped in bargeloads of manure and soap ash to improve the light sandy soil. When his son Charles inherited the island, he continued the improvements and made a pheasantry near the north shore, called Venetia Park, where he also built an ornamental cottage for the keeper. He was an MP for Bridport at the time.

In 1798, defensive strength was increased to protect the island from smugglers. Charles was appointed captain of the 150 strong Brownsea Island Artillery Volunteers, who manned the guns, four of which were on the castle terrace. Later, in 1842, a complete Coastguard Station was built to house the Chief Officer, his coastguards and their families. The station, which is now the National Trust café, was built to keep smuggling under control.

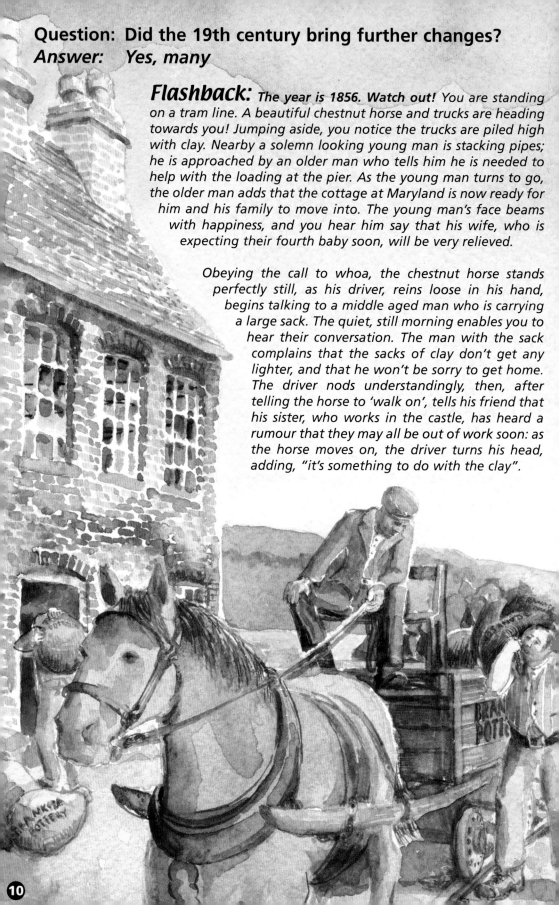

Question: Did the 19th century bring further changes?
Answer: Yes, many

Flashback: *The year is 1856. Watch out!* You are standing on a tram line. A beautiful chestnut horse and trucks are heading towards you! Jumping aside, you notice the trucks are piled high with clay. Nearby a solemn looking young man is stacking pipes; he is approached by an older man who tells him he is needed to help with the loading at the pier. As the young man turns to go, the older man adds that the cottage at Maryland is now ready for him and his family to move into. The young man's face beams with happiness, and you hear him say that his wife, who is expecting their fourth baby soon, will be very relieved.

Obeying the call to whoa, the chestnut horse stands perfectly still, as his driver, reins loose in his hand, begins talking to a middle aged man who is carrying a large sack. The quiet, still morning enables you to hear their conversation. The man with the sack complains that the sacks of clay don't get any lighter, and that he won't be sorry to get home. The driver nods understandingly, then, after telling the horse to 'walk on', tells his friend that his sister, who works in the castle, has heard a rumour that they may all be out of work soon: as the horse moves on, the driver turns his head, adding, "it's something to do with the clay".

When Colonel Waugh and his wife Mary viewed the island in 1852, Mary was struck by the purity of the clay, and convinced it would be suitable for the manufacture of porcelain. A professional geologist confirmed Mary's opinion, and suggested the clay was worth around a million pounds. Eager to buy, the Colonel paid £13,000 for the island and borrowed a vast amount of money to develop it. He had the Clock Tower built, the schoolhouse, the lovely church of St Mary of the Virgin and The Villa for the resident vicar. Another of Waugh's projects was to reclaim a hundred acres of land at St Andrew's Bay for meadowland, which was enclosed by a sea wall, constructed of a million bricks.

But the main reason for buying the island was for the industrial development, which Waugh called The Branksea Clay and Pottery Company. A large well equipped three storey pottery was built on the south west coast of the island. Three hundred yards west of this a terra-cotta and architectural pottery was built, where chimney pots, fire bricks and a more ornate type of ware was made; by the large pottery there were brickworks and drying sheds. Horse-drawn trucks transported the clay by tramway from the north shore to the new pier at the westernmost part of the island. The Colonel also had a village built at the north west corner of the island for some of his two hundred workers. Waugh named the village after his wife: Maryland consisted of four blocks of four houses. For the local people who lived and worked on the island this was a happy time, as both good working conditions and housing were hard to come by during the 19th century.

Sadly this busy, happy period did not last long; when it was discovered that the clay was not pure enough for porcelain, rumours spread and before long the Colonel was declared bankrupt, and he and his wife fled to Spain. For several years the mortgagees continued to keep the potteries open until a suitable buyer could be found. In 1871 The Honourable George Cavendish – Bentinck MP bought the island for £30,000, and continued the pottery production until, in 1887, it finally closed.

In his bid to make the island a viable community once again, Mr Cavendish-Bentinck concentrated on improving the agriculture of the island, bringing in pedigree stock and cultivating the arable land. A pub was opened, and became known as The Bentinck Arms.

As an art collector, Cavendish-Bentinck filled the castle with Italian Renaissance sculpture: some of it can still be seen today in the church and on the quay buildings. When Mr Cavendish-Bentinck died in 1891, the island was up for sale once more. The next owner was Major Kenneth Balfour MP, whose time on the island was saddened by his wife's illness and a disastrous fire in the castle in 1896. After rebuilding the castle, which included modern fire hydrants, Balfour put the island up for sale in 1901.

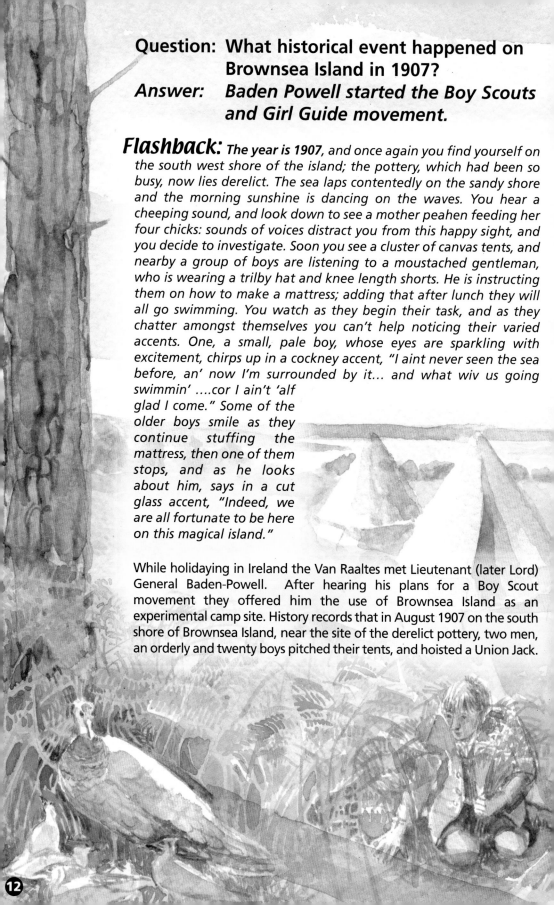

Question: What historical event happened on Brownsea Island in 1907?

Answer: *Baden Powell started the Boy Scouts and Girl Guide movement.*

Flashback: *The year is 1907, and once again you find yourself on the south west shore of the island; the pottery, which had been so busy, now lies derelict. The sea laps contentedly on the sandy shore and the morning sunshine is dancing on the waves. You hear a cheeping sound, and look down to see a mother peahen feeding her four chicks: sounds of voices distract you from this happy sight, and you decide to investigate. Soon you see a cluster of canvas tents, and nearby a group of boys are listening to a moustached gentleman, who is wearing a trilby hat and knee length shorts. He is instructing them on how to make a mattress; adding that after lunch they will all go swimming. You watch as they begin their task, and as they chatter amongst themselves you can't help noticing their varied accents. One, a small, pale boy, whose eyes are sparkling with excitement, chirps up in a cockney accent, "I aint never seen the sea before, an' now I'm surrounded by it… and what wiv us going swimmin' ….cor I ain't 'alf glad I come." Some of the older boys smile as they continue stuffing the mattress, then one of them stops, and as he looks about him, says in a cut glass accent, "Indeed, we are all fortunate to be here on this magical island."*

While holidaying in Ireland the Van Raaltes met Lieutenant (later Lord) General Baden-Powell. After hearing his plans for a Boy Scout movement they offered him the use of Brownsea Island as an experimental camp site. History records that in August 1907 on the south shore of Brownsea Island, near the site of the derelict pottery, two men, an orderly and twenty boys pitched their tents, and hoisted a Union Jack.

Helped by his friends Major Maclaren and Sir Arthur Pearson, Baden-Powell's experiment was under way, and he began to teach the boys scouting games, which he had taught himself as a boy. Some of the boys came from the local Boys Brigade in Poole, and it was their officer who collected together in advance all the materials and supplies for the camp. Other boys came from Eton, Harrow, and London's East End. Physical training and prayers followed breakfast, after which the troop was split into four Patrols; Curlews, Ravens, Wolves and Bulls. As well as swimming, they learnt craftwork, mattress making, how to live in the open, and to cook their own meals. Their powers of observation and comradeship developed as they learnt how to follow a trail, how to find a few grains of corn in an acre of heather and how to hide and find messages in trees. The days ended around a camp fire, where Baden-Powell would tell adventure stories, imitate the calls of birds and lead the Eengonyama chorus, which has been adopted by the Boy Scouts.

Inspired by the success of the camp, Baden-Powell finished his book 'Scouting for Boys', which led to scout troops being set up all over the country; by 1947, 4.4 million had joined. Later, Girl Guide groups were formed, and today young people throughout the world still model their activities on the camp set up in 1907 on Brownsea Island. Today, near the spot of the first campsite a monument has been erected to commemorate this historical event. In 1961, twenty years after his death, a Baden-Powell House was opened in London. Two years later, on Brownsea Island, Lady Olave Baden-Powell, his widow, addressed members of the Scout and Guide movement, and planted a mulberry tree outside the church. The day was one of great celebrations, more of which can be read about later in the history.

When you visit the Baden-Powell campsite on Brownsea, don't forget to have your letters and postcards stamped, before posting them on the island.

Question: What was life like on the island in the 20th century?

Answer: *Initially very happy.*

Flashback: *You feel yourself being pushed back once more.* It is the early 20th century. You find yourself in a cosy square room; a fire burns brightly at one end, with a black kettle hissing and steaming at the side. Along another wall is a large dresser, where a petite lady is reaching for one of the many jars on the top shelf. There is a wonderful aroma of baking bread.

A young boy dashes into the room and picks up a freshly cooked roll. He tells the lady he will see her at dinner time and leaves by a nearby door; you feel bound to follow. It is a cold, frosty morning and you begin to shiver. He joins five more children, chattering happily as they walk and skip along. Suddenly a gunshot is fired and the pungent aroma of gunpowder fills the air. Feeling alarmed you look at the children, who, unperturbed by the sound, peer through a gap in the trees. Curious, you join them and watch as a handful of men, all dressed in smart green outfits, aim their guns at various wildly flapping pheasants. The sound of splashing water directs your attention to a lake, where a man is directing his small craft to a certain spot, where he thrusts his hand in the icy water. Amid the mingled voices, one man shouts out, "Is there one down?" Triumphantly, the man in the boat holds up a lifeless pheasant. You hear one of the children say, "pheasant pie for tea again", and as the group continue on their way, you pass a cart, which is half filled with dead pheasants. A man comes out of the wood; as he flings more birds in the cart, he catches sight of the younger boy and you hear him say, "No time for dawdling Charlie, or you'll be late for school again." As you run to keep pace with the happy group, you realise school is not a place to be feared.

In 1901 Marcus van Raalte purchased Brownsea Island for his son, Charles, who had fallen in love with the island. Charles was a gentleman and very generous to the islanders, who all enjoyed an idyllic life under his care. Charles and his wife Florence furnished the castle tastefully, making it a beautiful home where they entertained many guests, including grand children and great grandchildren of Queen Victoria. The guests were transported to the island on the van Raalte's private steam launch, 'Blunderbuss'. In order to entertain his guests, Van Raalte formed a band, which played on the castle lawn during the social season. Prospective employees were always asked if they could play a musical instrument: this was very important as the band was made up of estate workers. You can still see a tuba from the band in the Visitor Centre.

Also during the Van Raalte's time a nine-hole golf course and a pheasant shoot were set out in the grounds. The island keepers were involved in the large shooting parties, and some of the estate workers helped as beaters and loaders:

all wore a smart uniform of hunting green. A boat was manned ready to catch any pheasants which fell into the lake.

Hothouses, a vinery, and a kitchen garden were built, which produced every type of fruit, including exotic fruits such as peaches, nectarines and grapes. You can still find the ruins today. With dairy products and meat being supplied by their own herds, Brownsea Island was virtually self sufficient during the Edwardian period. This was a good time for the workers and their families; they lived their lives in a happy and secure way: everything they needed was on the island, including the school, which was next to the Clock Tower.

In 1908, at the age of fifty, Charles van Raalte died. Although sad, the islanders' life under the care of Mrs van Raalte continued in the same blissful way. Unfortunately for them, this happiness was not to last, for in 1914 at the outbreak of World War 1, thirty of the islanders went to fight for their country. Only six returned.

Question: Were there any industries on the island during the 20th century?

Answer: Yes, the daffodil industry.

Flashback: *The year is 1912, and you find yourself high above the south shore in a field of beautiful daffodils; their sweet scent fills the air of the still spring evening. As you look around you are thrilled to see a sika deer grazing in a glade a few yards away. A group of adults and children are nearby; some are bent over, some are crouched, all intent on their task of picking the daffodils. For a while no one speaks; the only sound is the snapping of the picked stalks. Then, some teenage boys join them and the air is alive with chatter. You hear one lady asking the boys where her son is: a cheerful lad tells her that he is still in choir practise. As the lady continues to pick the daffodils, you hear her say that she hopes he won't be long as it will soon be dark, and besides, the extra money he can earn will help pay for his new uniform.*

Shortly before his death in 1908, Charles van Raalte had given instructions that a large part of the island was to be planted with daffodils. Developed by a grower from the Scilly Isles, it soon became a thriving business. The daffodils were mainly grown in the plateau above the south shore. Once distributed to the cottagers on the island, the cut flowers were tied into bunches, then stored before being loaded on to a boat and taken to Poole, from there they would be transported to the market at Covent Garden in London. Many of the islanders were involved, including the older children who helped to pick the flowers and distribute them.

The daffodil industry provided work throughout the year. After the last daffodils had been bunched, it was time to raise the bulbs, sort and replant them: following this, during the winter months packing cases were made in preparation for the following spring when the cycle would begin all over again.

In 1925, Mrs van Raalte decided to leave Brownsea. The island was bought by Sir Arthur Wheeler, who, after having had his plans for a country club and yacht haven turned down, put the island up for sale.

In 1927, Mrs Bonham Christie bought Brownsea Island as a retreat. Her ownership brought an end to the previously well managed estate, the daffodil industry, and the whole way of life.

Question: Why did life on the island have to change?
Answer: *A new owner had new ideas.*

Flashback: *The air becomes black as the decades unfold. You begin to cough as smoke fills your lungs: It is 1934 and a huge fire is engulfing the island. You realise that you are on the north side of the island, and run quickly towards the quay. You become breathless and are forced to slow down; a sense of panic grips you, for the air is filled with desperate voices and cries for help. Then suddenly the cries are lost amid the deafening sound of squeals. Now close to the quayside, you stand terrified and transfixed as scores of animals run past you towards the water. You pray to leave this time. Whoosh: Opening your eyes, you find it is a week later; you are still on the island, this time near the church. The ground is burnt and smouldering. Two fire fighters are close by observing the scene. One of them says that it is a mercy the church and castle were saved, adding that it was all due to the long hours put in by all those who helped.*

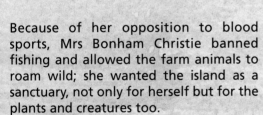

Because of her opposition to blood sports, Mrs Bonham Christie banned fishing and allowed the farm animals to roam wild; she wanted the island as a sanctuary, not only for herself but for the plants and creatures too.

This was a very sad time for the estate workers, who were forced to leave their beloved island and homes.

The old way of life, including the daffodil fields, was completely abandoned, leaving the island to revert to natural heathland once again.

Intent on keeping the island for her solitude, Mrs Christie banned all visitors, including the boy scouts, from the island. Brownsea gradually became an overgrown wilderness, which must have helped to spread the awful, raging fire which swept the island in July 1934, and burnt for a whole week. The Poole Fire Brigade and others worked for days trying to put out the fire, which could be seen for many miles. Thankfully the castle and church were saved, but tragically, many of the animals which Mrs Christie had tried to protect died in the fire. As the blaze spread across the island all that could be heard was the frightened squeal of the animals as they fled to the water.

Question: What role did the island play in World War II?
Answer: A vital one.

Flashback: *It is July1940: you find yourself in a large tent, which is full of women and children. Although crowded, the only noise is from a small baby, who is crying in its mother's arms; the mother talks quietly to her offspring; her words are in a strange tongue, as are those now spoken by an elderly lady, who is patting the ground and groaning. As the old lady pulls her blanket over her, the young mother speaks softly to the lady and strokes her hair. You watch this poignant scene until suddenly you are pushed forward. It is 1942, you are sitting near the edge of the cliff; it is very dark and quiet, except for the sound of the sea lapping the shoreline. As your eyes adjust to the light, you look around, but cannot recognise anything except the wiry grass beneath you. Suddenly the whole area is lit up; then a distant droning sound is heard. As the noise comes nearer and nearer, you begin to feel very anxious, and desperate for somewhere to hide. Once more you look about you, but not seeing any shelter, decide to stay where you are. The droning sound becomes louder and louder, you cover your ears and crouch as low as you can. Then, as the noise becomes unbearable, you feel compelled to look up, and see an aeroplane so close to you that you can almost see the pilot's face... you know he is the enemy. More aeroplanes follow; then comes the loudest bang imaginable and the whole area is lit up as flames leap high into the air. You want to run, but fear keeps you rooted to the spot. More explosions and flames light up the whole coastline. You pray that it will soon be over: then, gradually, gradually, the planes fly out to sea, the noise ceases, the darkness returns, and all is quiet once more.*

In contrast with the previous twelve years, the island was a busy place during the six years of World War II.

In May 1940, when the Germans invaded their countries, Dutch and Belgian people escaped on boats. Many of the 3,000 refugees, who had been directed into Poole harbour by the Royal Navy, found a safe temporary home on Brownsea Island. Mrs Bonham-Christie made the refugees welcome; and soon soup kitchens, washing troughs and lavatories were being assembled. The hastily installed refugee camp was manned by local people including the Girl Guides and Mrs Bonham-Christie, who helped with the preparation of the food. The refugees slept on the ground in marquees, which were erected on the Church field, and were allocated one blanket each: women and children in one marquee, and men in another. Once checked, which took weeks rather than days, the refugees were sent to the mainland.

Six inch guns were placed on Battery Hill to protect the entrance to Poole Harbour, and were manned by troops who stayed on the island throughout the war. Many cottages were used to house the military men and their stores;

the Guard Room was where the National Trust Reception area is today.

Brownsea also acted as a decoy island during the war. Navy personnel set up and operated decoy sites on the north western side of the island. Their purpose was to divert the enemy bombers away from Poole, and the cordite factory at Holton Heath. Various techniques were used to create fire, explosions and smoke to fool the enemy. Flares were sent up at night to distract the enemy planes, and in May 1942, in the safety of their concrete bunkers, the Navy personnel were given orders to stand by;

German bombers had been traced and were heading straight for Poole. The enemy bombs hit decoyed oil drums, and the explosions rocked the island.

Although Brownsea had suffered, including Maryland, which was left in ruins, Poole and Holton Heath were safe. Some of the bomb craters and bunkers can still be seen today.

Camouflaged as sheds, searchlights were installed in the South West corner of the castle grounds, and in the garden of the Villano: their purpose was to detect any enemy activity at sea.

Nearing the end of the war, it must have been an awesome sight to witness the 320 vessels leaving the harbour on the 4th June 1944, as they headed for the French coast for the D-Day landings.

Question: When was the island finally in safe hands?
Answer: In 1962, after many anxious months and rumours.

Flashback: *The year is 1961. You feel dizzy, sick, and confused. You are squashed into a tiny space; a loud whirring noise deafens you. Peeping cautiously, you see two pairs of feet and lots of dials, then realise you are in the cockpit of a helicopter! Male voices are heard; although much of the conversation is lost, you manage to catch some of it. Two men are discussing a certain project; one of them, who is very excited, urges his friend to look down, adding that it is the perfect spot for a marina, and will soon be all his. Feeling curious, you pull yourself up and peep through the low window; below you is a wonderful panoramic view of Brownsea Island. Then suddenly you start to feel dizzy and sick all over again.*

Following the war, Mrs Bonham-Christie resumed her life of isolation until 1961, when on the 28th April, at the age of 98, she passed away. Rumours circulated about the island's future, and many anxious months followed. It had been Mrs Bonham-Christies's wish that Brownsea be kept as a sanctuary for wildlife, but in order to meet death duties, her grandson had to put the island up for sale.

One man had plans drawn up for a marina; thankfully they were turned down. Rumours of luxury homes and a holiday camp were also heard at this time. Concerned for the island's future, local people formed the Brownsea Island Appeal Committee: their main aim was to protect the island from modern intrusions. A group of volunteers became the Brownsea Island Voluntary Wardens who patrolled the island and helped to look after it.

After a while the Treasury accepted the island in lieu of death duties, and the National Trust agreed to take it on provided that £100,000 was raised. Donations came from all over the country, including local businesses and individuals, who worked very hard on the project. Within six months the £100,000 had been raised: a wonderful effort from people wishing to preserve the uniqueness of Brownsea Island. Scouts and Guides and The Dorset Wildlife Trust helped too. Another kind donor was The John Lewis Partnership, who rented the castle from The National Trust, and used it as a hotel for its employees. By May 1962, after twelve months of uncertainty, Brownsea Island was safe.

A huge amount of work was undertaken, before the public could be welcomed to the island. Many dedicated volunteers and staff worked long hours at the arduous tasks. For safety reasons, the ruined cottages at Maryland had to be demolished, along with other dangerous buildings.

The overgrown wilderness of ivy, brambles and rhododendron had to be cleared to make paths and firebreaks. Other work undertaken included cleaning the inside of St Mary's Church.

The National Trust received help from other sources too, including The Dorset Naturalists Trust (now The Dorset Wildlife Trust) who leased over one third of the island to manage as a reserve.

Finally, after overcoming many obstacles, including the long, freezing winter of 1962/63, the island was ready to welcome visitors.

The opening ceremony was performed on the 16th May 1963 by Lady Olave Baden-Powell, chief of the World Wide Girl Guide movement, and widow of Lord Baden-Powell, founder of the Boy Scouts. On that happy day as long as you had 2/6d (12 and a half pence), you could land on the island, which for many years had been forbidden territory, and discover its many delights.

Question: What happened to the island after The National Trust took over?
Answer: It became a 'living island' once again.

You are shivering with the cold. The year is 1963. You are not sure which part of the island you are on; everywhere is covered with snow. Some men are working nearby; their breaths swirl about them as they chatter and laugh. One man, who is working with a hook, says that although clearing this wilderness is hard work in wintertime, it will be worth it, to have the island restored to its former glory once again.

WHOOSH: You are pushed forward; the temperature rises, and warmth seeps into your every pore. On your left, a smart lady is making a speech. She is surrounded by many people, all with happy, smiling faces; you recognise one man, who is clapping enthusiastically, and realise he is the man who was working with the hook on that cold, wintry day. As loud cheers fill the air, you feel lifted with the sense of happiness.

Question:
What is happening to Brownsea in the 21st Century?
Answer:
Conservation and Management.

To care for Brownsea in modern times, the island cannot be left to nature as in Mrs Bonham-Christie's era. If left to itself it would quickly revert to scrub.

The thousands of visitors, whose admission fees help to pay for the island's upkeep, need to be looked after as well. To this end, the National Trust designs and distributes visitors' leaflets, and organises family events and guided tours.

The woodlands on the island are home to the famous red squirrels – they rely especially on the pine trees for food. Staff and volunteers manage the woodlands by cutting down rhododendrons to let new pine trees grow, thus ensuring that there will be plenty of pine nuts for the squirrels.

The heather needs managing too – every thirty years it has a haircut to keep it young and healthy. Dorset Wildlife Trust looks after the birds on the lagoon by controlling the level of water. Look out for the artificial islands they have built for terns to nest on.

The lovely buildings on Brownsea don't look after themselves either! They always need repairs and some need a lot of conservation to stop them from falling down.

You can see that there are always decisions to be made about what to do next. One very difficult problem is what to do about global warming, which is causing sea levels to rise and might flood the lagoon with sea water. Making these decisions is the job of the Property Manager, the staff and volunteers. In their position, what would you do?

Question:
How can I help to look after Brownsea Island?
Answer:
By being thoughtful.

Brownsea Island is a beautiful place: with your help and thoughtfulness it will remain so.

Always take your litter home with you: not only does it look awful, it can be dangerous to wildlife.

Be careful with matches: fire can be devastating to wildlife.

Because Brownsea is a sanctuary for wildlife, no dogs, apart from guide dogs, are allowed on the island.

The island's habitats are fragile: we need to respect this, and also to be aware and respectful of other visitors. Although only a few people live on the island, the National Trust welcomes thousands of visitors each year, in contrast to 1854, when three hundred parishioners lived on the island, with only a few visitors landing each year.

By visiting Brownsea you are helping to support it. You can also help in other ways. By becoming a member of the National Trust on the island, you will contribute to its work here. Any money you spend in the Café or Gift shop will also help the Trust's activities on the island.

Brownsea Island would not survive without its willing volunteers. If you would like to join them, please contact a member of staff.

Pine Woodlands and Squirrels

Brownsea is famous for its red squirrels. They are increasingly rare in Britain: The Isle of Wight and the islands in Poole Harbour are the only places where they survive in Southern England. The squirrels especially like the Scots pine woodlands on Brownsea – they feed on the seeds in pine cones. These shy animals can be seen all year round, but are easiest to see in the autumn, when they are busy looking for nuts and seeds to store away for the winter; also in the early morning when they are most active. If you are very quiet and look up into the trees you might be lucky enough to see one or more.

Look Out for partly eaten cones: the Scots pinecone is smaller than the maritime pines.

Look Out in the more open areas for woodpeckers, and other birds which feed and nest on the trunks of the old dead trees.

Look Up to the top branches of the old pines, on the northern side in Oxford Wood: here herons nest on the top branches. You may also see sparrowhawks and buzzards.

Look Out for the big heaps of pine needles and other materials created by wood ants.

Mixed Woodlands and Sika Deer

The mixed woodland can be found in the central valley of the island; here many species of trees can be found, including oak, beech, sweet chestnut and hazel. Rhododendron is found growing in the woodland too. This plant is beautiful when it is flowering, but is a serious problem, as it prevents the natural regeneration of trees. Staff and volunteers manage the woodland by cutting down the rhododendron to allow young trees to grow. The sika deer hide during the day in woodlands or in the reedbeds. These shy creatures were introduced to Brownsea from Japan in 1896. Roe and fallow deer were also on the island until the awful fire in 1934, when all the deer swam to the mainland. During the 1970s the sika deer swam back to the island, and numbers have increased since then. Autumn is their mating season when their eerie cries can be heard at dawn and dusk.

Look Out for the frayed bark where the stags' antlers mark their territory.

GREEN WOODPECKER

NUTHATCH

Heath

Heath, which used to be very common in this part of Dorset and southern England is now a very rare habitat in Europe. The most common plants are heathers, which are especially beautiful when they flower in July and August. Heath is a man made landscape – if the area is not managed it would return to woodland. On Brownsea different areas of heath are cut every year. This encourages new heather to grow. **Look Out** for these patches of cut heath on the island.

Look Out for lizards, dragonflies and a variety of butterflies, including the small copper, common blue, silver studded blue and green hairstreak, which are attracted to the heath.

If you visit on warmer days **Look Out** for the green tiger beetles, and the common lizard.

Nesting among the older growth are sallow warblers and dunnocks: as with all the wildlife, please take care not to disturb them.

If you should be fortunate enough to be on the island in the evening, you might hear and see the nightjar, a visitor from Africa. The nightjar nests in the heathy parts of the island and flies late in the evening in summer, performing its curious 'churring' call and wing clapping courtship displays.

WILLOW WARBLER

OYSTERCATCHER

DUNNOCK

NIGHTJAR

REEPER

Peacocks

The beautiful peacocks, whose distinctive call echoes throughout the island, were probably introduced to Brownsea during the Edwardian period, as ornamental birds. If you are very fortunate you might see the male peacock's long iridescent tail feathers form a fan shape, which is part of his courtship display.

Watch out though, they can peck if you get too close!

25

The Lagoon

The Brownsea Lagoon is home for a huge variety of birds throughout the year. The Lagoon, which was reclaimed from the harbour in the 1850s, was neglected during Mrs Bonham- Christie's time, thus creating a rich, non-tidal wetland, attracting birds especially adapted to feed in brackish water and mudflats.

If you visit in the spring or autumn, you might see waders migrating to and from their northern nesting sites.

Look Out for curlew sandpiper, greenshank, black and bar tailed godwit, curlew, sanderling, spotted redshank, and ruff.

Many birds over-winter here and at high tide thousands feed here.

Look Out for the tiny dunlin, which feeds in the shallow water, and the avocet, which strides through the deeper water, sweeping its upturned bill from side to side, catching its prey.

Around the edges of the lagoon **Look Out** for teal, Brownsea's smallest duck. Also **Look Out** for cormorants roosting on the sand spits, and wheatears and kingfishers, which are a common sight here.

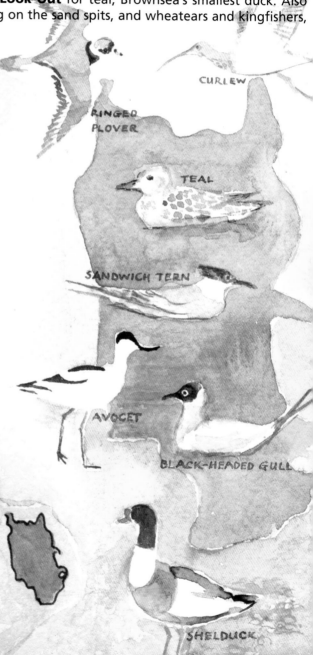

CURLEW

RINGED PLOVER

TEAL

SANDWICH TERN

AVOCET

BLACK-HEADED GULL

SHELDUCK

April is a busy time at the Lagoon as the over–wintering birds leave and the summer birds arrive from Africa and southern Europe.

Listen Out for the wonderful harsh cries of the returning common and sandwich terns: from May to July if you go to the Dorset Wildlife Trust bird watching hides **Look Out** for the specially made gravel islands where the terns feed their young on small fish, sand eels and shrimps. Since these islands were made, the number of breeding terns has grown dramatically. Little terns visit in spring and late summer, but do not breed.

Shelducks, which nest under stumps and in old burrows in the wood, live here all the year round; unfortunately their ducklings and mallard ducklings are heavily predated by gulls, crows and magpies.

Look Out for the introduced Canada geese and their goslings, which are to be found on the church meadow.

While at the Lagoon **Look Out** for grey herons and little egrets, which feed there. Brownsea was the first place in Britain where the little egret nested.

The Fresh Water Marsh, Lakes and Reedbeds

In the central valley, Brownsea drains into two lakes. Sallow (another name for pussy and goat willow) and alder carr trees grow around the reedbeds where common reed has invaded the old meadows, which flooded during Mrs Bonham-Christie's time. Among these reeds you might be really lucky and see water voles. **Listen Out** for the plop of a water vole entering the water. The alder trees are an important source of seed for over-wintering birds such as siskin, redpoll, and goldfinch: the carr supports flocks of blue, great marsh and long-tailed tits.

If you visit in the summer **Listen Out** for the harsh chatter of the reed warbler, which lives and feeds upon the reedbeds. Between April and July **Listen Out** for the cuckoo, who seeks out the reed warbler's nest in which to lay her own eggs. Reed bunting, moorhen and mallard breed here each year.

Look Out for delicate wild flowers around the marsh edge: you could see marsh orchid, ragged robin, lady's smock,

gipsywort, marsh pennywort, bog pimpernel and marsh bird's foot trefoil. Many spiders over-winter in the hollow stems, and sallows are food for hundreds of insects including puss moth, buff tip and the scarce lunar hornet clearwing, whose caterpillar lives for two years inside the trunk.

Not many fish can live in the water of the lakes, which is quite acidic, but **Look Out** for sticklebacks, diving beetles, damselflies and dragonflies. Up to fifty tufted ducks and a few pochard over-winter on them, and usually two pairs of little grebes stay to nest.

The larvae of the dragonfly lives underwater for months, sometimes years: Brownsea can boast up to twenty four different species, including the common blue damselfly, the scarce red damselfly, the four spotted chaser, the ruddy darter and the southern hawker.

If you visit in the autumn **Look Out** for sika deer, which are regularly seen in the marsh. **Look Out** for stripped sallows, a sign that the deer have been feeding or where stags have rubbed the bark with their antlers in the autumn mating season.

G-TAILED TIT

MALLARD

TUFTED DUCK

D WARBLER

MOORHEN

WATER VOLE

The Seashore

Just like the rest of Brownsea Island, the seashore is not only beautiful but an important habitat: take time to explore it. Poole Harbour is very important for its wildlife: especially the thousands of birds which feed and breed here. The mud and sand might not look very interesting, but it is full of things for birds to eat.

As you walk along the seashore **Look Out** for the strandline – things washed up by the tide and left at high water mark. Sandhoppers feed on the washed up seaweed – **Look Out** for them, especially if you turn some of the seaweed over. At low tide you might see the serrated wrack with its jagged edges and bladder wrack with its bubbly fronds. **Look Out** for shells washed up on the shore – cockles, razor shells and others. These live in the mud and sand in the harbour and are an important food source for the birds. **Look Out** too for the Manilla clam, which was introduced to the harbour for the fishing industry.

Look Out for oystercatchers, which nest on the shingle just above the high tide mark. Please tread carefully though, and **Look and Listen Out** for an agitated circling bird. This is a sign that you are too close to the nest.

The oystercatchers are the only waders seen here in the summer, but are joined in the winter months by redshanks and the common sandpiper.

Look Out for turnstones searching for invertebrates along the strandline. During the winter months Brownsea attracts many birds from colder countries. **Look Out** on the water for eider duck, goldeneye, great-crested and Slavonian grebes, red-breasted merganser and divers.

CURLEW

RED-THROATED DIVER

COMMON SANDPIPER

REDSHANK

EIDER DRAKE

OYSTER CATCHER

TURNSTONE

RED-BREASTED MERGANSER

GOLDENEYE

SANDHOPPER